EDGE
BOOKS

DIRT BIKES

Dirt Bike History

by Terri Sievert

Consultant:

Dirck J. Edge
Editor
MotorcycleDaily.com

Capstone
press

Mankato, Minnesota

Edge Books are published by Capstone Press
151 Good Counsel Drive, P.O. Box 669, Mankato, Minnesota 56002
www.capstonepress.com

Library of Congress Cataloging-in-Publication Data
Sievert, Terri.
  Dirt bike history / by Terri Sievert.
    p. cm.—(Edge books. Dirt bikes)
  Summary: Describes the history of dirt bike competitions, including the major
events and athletes in the sport.
  Includes bibliographical references (p. 31) and index.
  ISBN 0-7368-2439-1 (hardcover)
  1. Supercross—History—Juvenile literature. 2. Trail bikes—History—Juvenile
literature. [1. Motocross. 2. Supercross. 3. Motorcycle racing. 4. Trail bikes.] I. Title.
II. Series.
  GV1060.1455.S54 2004
  796.6'3—dc22   2003013717

Editorial Credits

Angela Kaelberer, editor; Molly Nei, series designer; Jason Knudson, book designer;
    Jo Miller, photo researcher

Photo Credits

Anthony Scavo, 8
Corbis/Bettmann, 13; Gunter Marx Photography, 16; Hulton-Deutsch Collection,
    11, 15
Getty Images/Donald Miralle, 26; Elsa, 19; Francois Dubourg, 6; Robert Cianflone,
    cover
Kinney Jones Photography, 25
Ray Gundy, 29
Rene Kotopoulis, 20
SportsChrome-USA/Bongarts Photography, 24
Steve Bruhn, 5, 23

1 2 3 4 5 6 09 08 07 06 05 04

Table of Contents

CHAPTER 1

Motocross Racing

On January 15, 1994, Jeremy McGrath was racing his 250cc Honda at the Florida Citrus Bowl Stadium in Orlando. On the last jump, McGrath tried something different. As the bike was in midair, McGrath swung his right leg over the rear fender and past the bike's left footpeg. The crowd cheered McGrath's trick, which he later called the nac-nac.

Soon, other motocross riders began doing tricks during races. Fans liked the tricks so much that a new sport was born. Riders began competing in freestyle motocross contests.

Learn about:
- Freestyle tricks
- Early dirt bikes
- Races

Jeremy McGrath invented one of the first freestyle tricks, the nac-nac.

Freestyle motocross riders take dirt bike riding to the extreme. Not long ago, the bikes that sail through the air were used mainly for racing.

Some motocross races are held on sandy courses.

Dirt Bike Racing

People began racing motorcycles in the early 1900s. They raced up hills, on wooden tracks, and on flat dirt tracks. People also raced motorcycles in the open country. At first, these off-road races were called trials or scrambles. Later, people designed courses for off-road racing. They started to call the sport "motocross."

In the 1950s, motorcycle companies began to design and build motorcycles for riding on rough, bumpy off-road courses. People called these motorcycles "dirt bikes."

In the 1970s, people started racing dirt bikes in large sports arenas. This sport came to be known as supercross. Later, people held races in smaller arenas. These races are called arenacross.

Dirt bike riders also compete in other races. They still race on dirt tracks. They also ride in long off-road races called enduros and cross-country races. They race on tracks that are part dirt and part pavement in supermoto races.

Dirt bike engines create power for riders to do tricks.

Engines

Most motocross bikes have two-stroke engines. These engines have one hollow tube called a cylinder. Inside the cylinder, a piston moves up and down. The engines use two strokes of the piston to complete the fuel cycle. The engines take in fuel and air, compress the mixture, and set it on fire. They then release burned gas as exhaust.

A few dirt bikes have four-stroke engines. These engines use four piston strokes to operate. The two extra strokes allow four-stroke engines to run quieter and give off less exhaust than two-stroke engines.

The engine size of a dirt bike is measured in cubic centimeters (ccs). Most dirt bike racers ride motorcycles with 125cc or 250cc engines.

CHAPTER 2

Early Races

In Europe, early off-road races were called scrambles. Riders rode over rough, bumpy courses. In 1914, workers at the Scott Motorcycle Company in Yorkshire, England, raced on rough ground between the towns of Shipley and Bumsall. The Scott Trial is still held each year.

European riders continued to compete in scrambles during the 1920s and 1930s. The races were especially popular in Great Britain and France. People started calling the races "motocross." This word is a combination of motorcycle and cross-country.

Learn about:
- Scrambles
- European races
- Titles

Scrambles were popular in Europe during the 1930s.

World War II and Motocross

Motocross was popular in Europe, but few people in North America knew about the sport. Most early North American races took place on flat paved or dirt tracks.

Many U.S. and Canadian soldiers fought in Europe during World War II (1939–1945). The soldiers saw motocross races for the first time in Europe. Some soldiers organized races when they returned home, but the sport did not become popular right away.

Motocross Championships

In 1947, the Federation of International Motorcyclists (FIM) held the first Motocross des Nations. Teams of riders from many European countries competed in this motocross race in Paris, France. Great Britain's team won the event. The race has been held every year since then.

In 1957, the FIM began the World Motocross Championship Series. This race series was for individual riders instead of teams. Bill Nilsson from Sweden became the first world champion. Today, riders in the Unlimited, 250cc, and 125cc classes compete for this title.

This 1933 race was held at a flat dirt track in Compton, California.

CHAPTER 3

Modern Racing

In the 1950s, motorcycle companies in Europe built bikes for off-road racing. These cycles were called dirt bikes. To make the bikes lighter, designers removed the headlights and other unneeded parts. The bikes also had knobby tires that gripped the mud and dirt.

In the 1960s, Japanese motorcycle companies began building and improving dirt bikes. They developed smaller, more powerful engines. Honda, Suzuki, Yamaha, and Kawasaki made many popular bikes. These companies still make most dirt bikes.

Learn about:
- Bikes
- Supercross
- Freestyle

In the 1950s, riders raced the first bikes built for off-road racing.

Motocross in North America

In 1966, four-time world motocross champion Torsten Hallman came to the United States from Sweden. Hallman entered U.S. off-road races. He won most of them, including the Hopetown Grand Prix. This California race was the biggest U.S. off-road race at the time.

Motocross racing was popular in North America by the 1970s.

The next year, other European riders joined Hallman in the United States. Their races were known as the Inter-Am Series. Many people in the United States and Canada became interested in motocross.

The American Motorcyclist Association (AMA) started the National Championship Motocross Series in 1972. These races are now called the AMA Motocross Series.

Supercross

Until the early 1970s, all motocross races were held outdoors on large dirt tracks. Fans could not easily see the action that was not close to them.

In 1972, a motocross race was held in the Los Angeles Coliseum in California. A dirt course was built on the stadium field. Fans could see the action more easily than on a regular motocross track. The race was called the "Super Bowl of Motocross." People soon shortened this name to supercross.

In 1976, the AMA started the International Invitational Supercross Series. These races are now called the AMA Supercross Series.

Arenacross

Some motocross races are held in smaller arenas. These races are called arenacross. Outdoor races cannot be held during winter in many areas. Racers can compete on indoor arenacross tracks even during winter. In the United States, arenacross riders compete in the National Arenacross Series.

The winding arenacross tracks are about one-quarter mile (.4 kilometer) long. Most supercross tracks are about one-half mile (.8 kilometer) long.

Freestyle

In the 1990s, some racers started doing tricks at the end of races or between races. These racers started the sport of freestyle motocross. Freestyle riders do not race. Instead, judges score them on the difficulty and performance of their tricks.

Mike Metzger was one of the first racers to do freestyle tricks. In 2002, he and Travis Pastrana became the first riders to land backflips in competition without crashing. Kenny Bartram, Mike Jones, and Carey Hart are other top freestyle riders.

Carey Hart is a top freestyle motocross rider.

Bob Hannah

Bob Hannah is one of the most successful motocross racers ever. His nickname is "Hurricane" Hannah.

Hannah was born in 1956 in California. He began riding dirt bikes at age 7. In 1974, 18-year-old Hannah entered his first amateur race and won. The next year, he turned pro.

In the late 1970s, Hannah won three AMA Motocross and three AMA Supercross Championships. During his career, he won 70 national AMA races, a record that stood until 1999. Hannah scored 27 of these wins in the 250cc class. This record stood until Ricky Carmichael broke it in 2000.

Hannah retired in 1989. In 1999, he became a member of the AMA Hall of Fame.

CHAPTER 4

Events

In 1972, the United States sent its first team to the Motocross des Nations race. Nine years later, the team of Donnie Hansen, Danny LaPorte, Johnny O'Mara, and Chuck Sun won the first championship for the United States. The U.S. team took home the first-place trophy every year until 1994, when it finished second. The United States won the race again in 1996 and 2000.

Learn about:

- World events
- Race series
- Supermoto

Ricky Carmichael, Ryan Hughes, and Travis Pastrana teamed to win the 2000 Motocross des Nations.

Supercross events are held in large arenas.

World Competitions

The world's top supercross and motocross riders compete in a series of races. World Supercross Championship races are held between January and May. Motocross riders compete in the World Motocross Championship Series. The races are held from May to September.

In 2003, Australian Chad Reed became the first World Supercross champion. He won nine of the 17 events in the series.

The motocross season runs from May to September.

Freestyle riders like Doug Parsons compete in the X Games.

Freestyle Competitions

In 1998, the International Freestyle Motocross Association (IFMA) formed. The IFMA holds more than 35 freestyle competitions each year.

Since 1999, freestyle riders also have competed in the X Games and the Gravity Games. The riders with the most points win medals and prize money.

Other Races

Today, motocross and supercross are the most popular off-road races. But some racers compete in other off-road races.

Enduro racing courses are often 40 to 80 miles (64 to 129 kilometers) long. Racers try to reach the end of the course in a set amount of time.

Land speed racers try to set speed records on dry lake beds or other large, flat areas of land. Engine size for these bikes ranges from 50cc to more than 3000cc.

Supermoto

Supermoto is a new form of racing. Some parts of the supermoto tracks are dirt. Other sections of the tracks are paved. The tracks have the jumps of motocross tracks and the sliding corners of dirt tracks.

Supermoto bikes are different from motocross bikes in several ways. Supermoto bikes are lower to the ground and have smaller wheels than motocross bikes. Supermoto tires are smoother than the knobby dirt bike tires. Supermoto tires are more like street bike tires, because the course has more paved sections than dirt.

Future of Dirt Bikes

Off-road racing has changed in many ways since the first scrambles of the early 1900s. Few people then could imagine that a rider would ever backflip a bike 40 feet (12 meters) into the air. In the future, dirt bike riders will keep setting new speed records and inventing even more daring tricks.

Supermoto tracks have both paved and dirt areas.

Glossary

cubic centimeter (KYOO-bik SENT-uh-mee-tur)— a unit that measures the size of a motorcycle engine; this unit is abbreviated "cc."

cylinder (SIL-uhn-dur)—a hollow area inside an engine in which fuel burns to create power

exhaust (eg-ZAWST)—the waste gases produced by a dirt bike engine

piston (PIS-tuhn)—a part inside an engine cylinder that moves up and down as fuel burns

scramble (SKRAM-buhl)—an off-road motorcycle race

supermoto (soo-puhr-MOH-toh)—a sport in which dirt bikes race on tracks with both paved and dirt areas

Read More

Freeman, Gary. *Motocross.* Radical Sports. Chicago: ...nemann Library, 2003.

Hendrickson, Steve. *Supercross Racing.* Motorcycles. Mankato, Minn.: Capstone Press, 2000.

Schaefer, A. R. *Motocross Cycles.* Wild Rides! Mankato, Minn.: Capstone Press, 2002.

Useful Addresses

American Motorcyclist Association
13515 Yarmouth Drive
Pickerington, OH 43147-8273

Canadian Motorcycle Association
P.O. Box 448
Hamilton, ON L8L 1J4
Canada

Motorcycle Safety Foundation
2 Jenner Street, Suite 150
Irvine, CA 92618-3806

Internet Sites

FactHound offers a safe, fun way to find Internet sites related to this book. All of the sites on FactHound have been researched by our staff.

Here's how:

1. Visit *www.facthound.com*
2. Type in this special code **0736824391** for age-appropriate sites. Or enter a search word related to this book for a more general search.
3. Click on the **Fetch It** button.

FactHound will fetch the best sites for you!

Index